Reading Maps

KEVIN CUNNINGHAM

Children's Press®
An Imprint of Scholastic Inc.
New York   Toronto   London   Auckland   Sydney
Mexico City   New Delhi   Hong Kong
Danbury, Connecticut

Content Consultant
Laura McCormick, Cartographer
XNR Productions
Madison, Wisconsin

Library of Congress Cataloging-in-Publication Data
Cunningham, Kevin, 1966–
  Reading maps/Kevin Cunningham.
      p. cm.—(A true book)
  Includes bibliographical references and index.
  ISBN-13: 978-0-531-26006-7 (lib. bdg.) — ISBN-13: 978-0-531-26237-5 (pbk.)
  1. Map reading—Juvenile literature. I. Title.
  GA130.C96 2012
  912.01'4—dc23   2012000692

Front cover: Maps displayed on handheld devices
Back cover: A folding tourist map

Find the Truth!

Everything you are about to read is true *except* for one of the sentences on this page.

Which one is **TRUE**?

T or F   Meridians are always the same distance apart.

T or F   The equator separates the Northern and Southern Hemispheres.

Find the answers in this book.

3

Contents

THE **BIG** TRUTH!

The Trouble with Longitude

4

An early
compass box

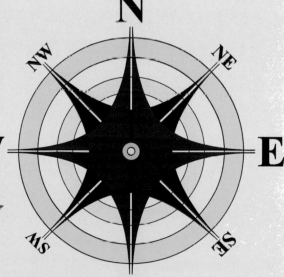

4 Reading the Legend

What kinds of information are found
in a map's legend?

5 Online Maps

What makes online maps different from
print maps?

The word "east"
comes from an
ancient word
meaning "dawn."

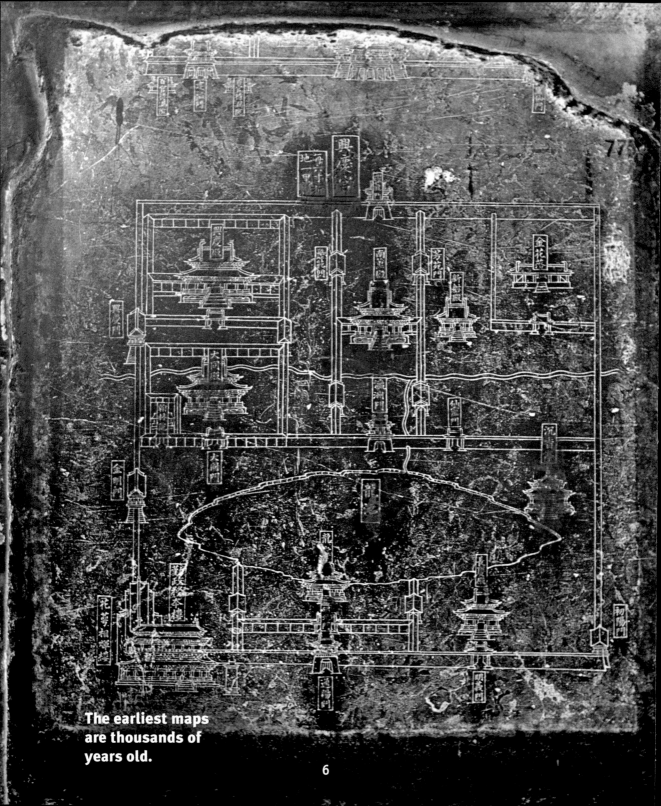

The earliest maps
are thousands of
years old.

CHAPTER 1

Making Sense of a Map

A map provides information about a place with pictures instead of words. Many people think of maps as being printed on paper, but this is not always true. Museums own Native American maps painted on animal skin, Middle Eastern maps etched into clay, and Polynesian maps made of sticks and shells. Today, many maps are found online. Whatever materials are used to make them, most maps share certain features.

In China, maps were sometimes carved into large polished marble pieces called steles.

Basic Elements

One easy-to-find feature is the title. This explains what information will be in the map. A signature by the **cartographer** may be another element. Some maps also have the year the map was made. The legend explains the symbols used on the map. The map's border, or neatline, surrounds the map and all the other elements. It marks where the map begins and ends. Other elements direct a reader around the map by showing directions and how to compute distances.

Titles on maps are often in large, bold letters to make them easy to find.

CENTRAL TŌKYŌ

Some world maps curve at the sides to prevent distortion of land sizes.

It is easy to recognize a world map.

Some maps note the kind of **projection** the cartographer chose to use. The projection transfers, or projects, the features of the round earth onto a flat surface such as a piece of paper. Projections change the shapes of the earth's features to make everything fit on a flat surface. There are countless different projections. Each distorts the earth differently. It is helpful to the reader to know what projection was used to avoid confusion.

A full compass rose
has 32 points.

CHAPTER 2

Finding Direction

No map can show all the details of the place it describes. Cartographers must make choices about what to put in and what to leave out. They make many other choices, too. One of the ways map users can find direction is by using the map's **orientation**. The orientation links the directions drawn on the map to directions in the real world. A map's orientation is given by an element called the **compass rose**.

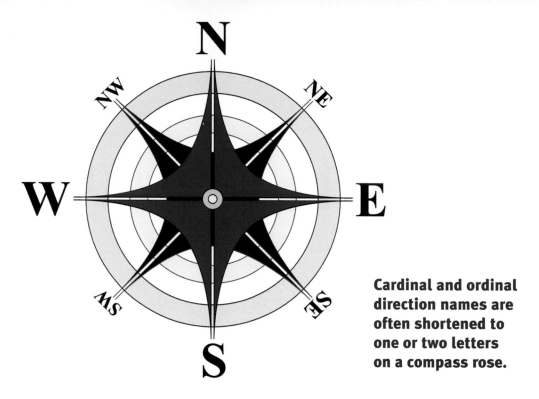

Cardinal and ordinal direction names are often shortened to one or two letters on a compass rose.

Points on the Rose

A compass rose's main points face north, south, east, and west. These are called the cardinal directions. They form a cross on the compass rose. Four ordinal directions—northeast, southeast, northwest, and southwest—form an X. Most compass roses show no more than these eight points. Other compass roses only show the four cardinal directions or just a single arrow pointing north.

To orient a map to the real world, a map reader first spreads the map out on a flat surface. Then she finds north (N) on the map's compass rose. From there, she turns to face the real north and lines up the N on the compass rose with the direction she's facing. When that's done, she has found the map's orientation. It's now possible to use the map, whether for travel or for other purposes.

A compass needle always points to the magnetic north pole.

A handheld compass comes in handy when orienting a map to the real world.

Which Way Is Up?

Cartographers today usually create maps with north at the top. The choice may seem like the "right" way. But it's a tradition, not a necessity. Maps used other orientation points for centuries. In the Middle Ages, Christians in Europe often drew east at the top of their maps. This was because east pointed in the direction of Jerusalem, Christianity's holiest city. Maps made in Japan were often drawn with the emperor's palace at the top.

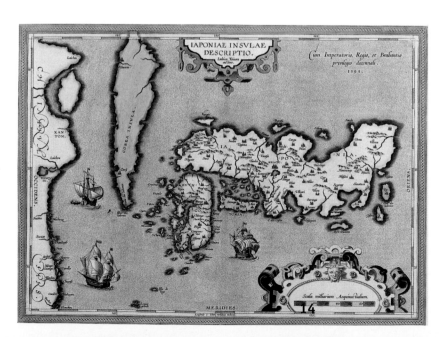

Maps were often oriented to a location of great importance, such as the Japanese emperor's palace.

The Ptolemaeus crater on Mars is named after the mapmaker Ptolemy.

Pointing North

Greek mapmaker Claudius Ptolemy is considered one of the fathers of cartography. In the second century CE, Ptolemy used mathematics to make maps that were unusually accurate for his time. He also oriented his maps with north pointing up. Many of Ptolemy's methods were lost until European mapmakers rediscovered his teachings in the 1400s. These mapmakers took Ptolemy's advice on orienting a map toward the north. As European ideas spread, mapmakers around the world adopted Ptolemy's tradition.

Other Orientations

Not everyone agrees with Ptolemy today. A kind of map called a reversed map places south at the top. This is to get people to see southern countries as being as important as Europe or North America. Other maps have to use different orientations. The South Pole sits in the center of a map of Antarctica. North is at the top, left, right, and bottom, because every place on the map lies north of the pole.

Antarctica sits at the top of a reversed map.

16

Changing the World

Centuries ago, people in China magnetized the tips of metal needles by touching them to magnetic rocks called lodestones. An early Chinese compass was a magnetized needle floating in water. In the 1200s, European craftsmen built a compass in a box. They painted a compass rose on a paper card placed underneath the needle. The sturdy boxed compass helped ships find their way. European sailors soon made longer journeys in search of fish, rare spices, and new lands.

Christopher Columbus used a magnetic compass.

A globe may represent Earth,
the moon, or any other sphere.

CHAPTER 3

Latitude and Longitude

Cartographers use a system of crossing lines to help map readers find locations on the earth. Lines running east and west show **latitude**. Lines of latitude run **parallel** around the earth. In fact, mapmakers refer to latitude lines as parallels. The parallels are always about 69 miles (111 kilometers) apart. The equator, also known as 0 degrees latitude, splits the earth into two **hemispheres**: northern and southern.

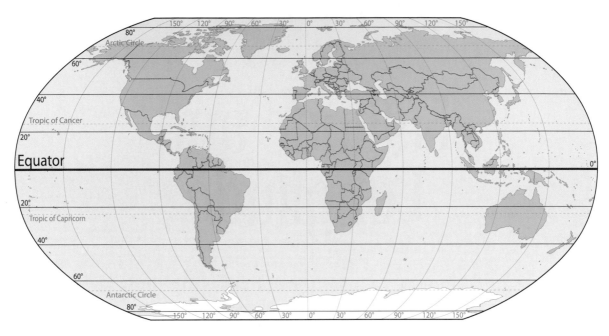

The equator is located at zero degrees.

Distance by Degrees

Maps divide these hemispheres into 90 degrees of latitude. Each line is numbered to show its distance north or south of the equator. A low latitude, such as 10 degrees south, runs near the equator. High latitudes cross far from the equator. The North Pole lies at 90 degrees north, usually written as 90° N. The South Pole lies at 90 degrees south, or 90° S.

Long Lines

Lines running north and south represent **longitude**. A line of longitude, or meridian, starts at the North Pole and ends at the South Pole. One line's distance from the next varies. The bulge of the earth pushes meridians farthest apart at the equator. As the lines move north or south they draw closer together and then connect at the poles. The prime meridian represents o degrees longitude. It splits the earth into two hemispheres: western and eastern.

The distance between longitude lines decreases as they near the poles.

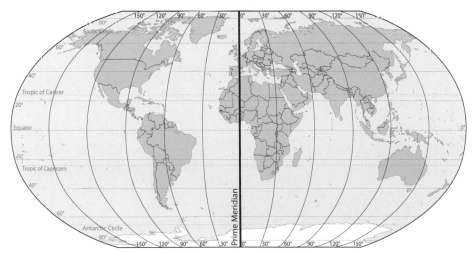

Maps divide the Western and Eastern Hemispheres into 180 degrees of longitude each. A meridian's number shows distance west or east. Low numbers run nearest the prime meridian. Both 180° E and 180° W—the highest numbers of longitude—share a line. That line runs through the Pacific Ocean exactly opposite the prime meridian. A traveler going east loses a day when crossing most of this line. A traveler adds a day going west.

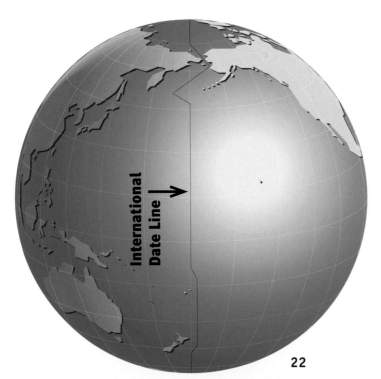

The line down 180° E and 180° W is called the International Date Line.

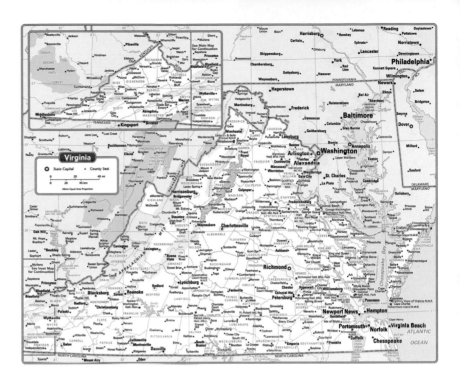

More than one degree of latitude and longitude intersect in Virginia.

Using Latitude and Longitude

Coordinates refer to which lines of latitude and longitude meet at a certain location. For example, Virginia is at 37° N and 78° W. But there is a lot of space between each degree of latitude and longitude. No degrees of latitude and longitude cross at Washington, D.C. In order to find the city, a map reader will need to divide degrees into smaller units.

Exact coordinates are important to soldiers in the field.

By the Numbers

To provide more exact coordinates, each degree of latitude and longitude is split into 60 measurements called minutes. Using minutes, a map reader can locate Washington, D.C., at 38 degrees and 53 minutes north, and 77 degrees and 2 minutes west. This can also be written as N 38°53' and W 77°2', with latitude always coming first.

Each minute of latitude and longitude contains 60 seconds. Seconds allow mapmakers to show coordinates for places as small as a building. For example, the Washington Monument stands at the coordinates N 38°53'22.27" and W 77°2'6.97". In other words, the latitude is 38 degrees, 53 minutes, and 22.27 seconds north (N) of the equator. The longitude is 77 degrees, 2 minutes, and 6.97 seconds west (W) of the prime meridian.

Coordinates make it easy to pinpoint the locations of important landmarks, such as the Washington Monument.

The Trouble with Longitude

By the late 1600s, a ship's **navigator** could find latitude by comparing the position of the sun to special charts. But navigators could not measure longitude. Without it, a ship could not locate its exact position moving east and west. In 1707, England's government formed the Board of Longitude to award money to whoever solved the longitude problem.

One idea was to keep a clock on a ship. The clock kept the time at a known meridian. This was compared to the ship's "local time," measured by the sun and the stars. By finding the difference, a captain could work out how far his ship had traveled. But a ship's rocking made the clocks inaccurate.

In 1759, carpenter and clock maker John Harrison invented a chronometer that would remain accurate at sea. The Board of Longitude wanted to make copies of Harrison's chronometer before granting the reward. Harrison fought the board, but agreed in 1765. He received half of the money then and most of the rest in 1773.

CHAPTER 4

Reading the Legend

A cartographer uses a legend, also called a key, to explain how to read the map. Complicated maps tend to have longer legends because there is more to explain. Often the largest part of the legend lists the symbols or pictures used by the mapmaker. Symbols have several uses. One is to pinpoint natural features and man-made landmarks. Common symbols for natural features include a small cross for a tall mountain and dots for a desert.

 City maps often mark popular places to visit.

Contour maps are helpful tools for mountain climbers and hikers.

The closer together lines on a contour map are, the steeper the real land is.

Flat but Three-Dimensional

A map is flat, but cartographers can use symbols to show the height of an area. On a contour map, a series of lines show the general shape of a mountain. An experienced map reader can study the distance between the lines and imagine the steepness of the mountainside. Similar symbols may show lowlands such as marshes and even the trenches at the bottom of the ocean.

Adding Color

A legend also decodes the colors used by the mapmakers. Water, for instance, is usually blue. Mountains may be dark brown, hills light brown, and deserts yellow. It's up to the cartographer. Some maps combine symbols with colors to pass along information. Green pine trees may show the borders of a forest. The same map might use different green symbols for treeless prairies, swamps, and rain forests.

This map uses colors and symbols to show things such as water, mountains, and trees.

Cartographers use color for very specific purposes, depending on the type of map being created. A map reader should study the legend to learn what each color on the map means. This avoids confusion. Take a map that uses dark brown. A map reader may have assumed brown means dry and barren. But the legend may state that brown refers only to the height of the land. The cartographer, in other words, is saying nothing about plant life.

Timeline of Orientation and Navigation

100s CE
Lodestones are used in compasses in China.

100s
Ptolemy produces maps oriented so that north is pointed up.

Man-Made Places

Road maps in particular use symbols for man-made landmarks. For instance, an airplane icon might mark an airport. The legend helps a reader decode the road system, too. Thick lines, thin lines, dotted lines, lines of many colors—all can be used to show anything from a horse trail to an eight-lane interstate highway. Shields, circles, and other shapes help the reader find specific road numbers, such as Route 90 or Interstate 10.

1400s
Making maps oriented to the north becomes popular in Europe.

1200s
The first compass boxes are built in Europe.

1759
John Harrison builds the first successful chronometer.

The Scale

A legend usually includes the scale for the map. The scale allows a map reader to measure a distance on the map and convert it to real-life miles or kilometers. Scales come in many forms. The commonly used bar scale shows a checkered line. On it, distances are marked every inch, every 5 centimeters, or at some other length easily measured by a ruler.

This map of Europe during World War I (1914–1918) uses a bar scale.

Because Earth is round, it is impossible for a map to be perfectly to scale.

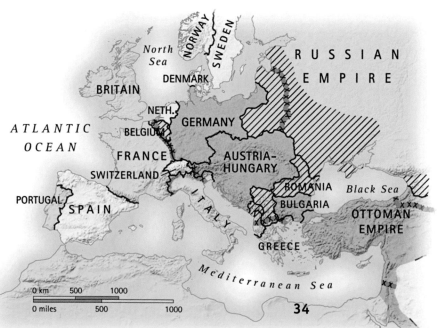

34

Distance on a map can be measured with a ruler and compared to the map's scale to find the real-life distance.

Numbers show that a certain length equals a certain real-life distance. One inch (2.54 cm) could equal 100 miles (161 km). Another type of scale does away with pictures. Words inside the legend simply explain the scale: "One inch equals 100 miles (161 km)." Scales on many government maps use only numbers. For example, the scale 1:63,360 means 1 inch (2.54 cm) on the map equals 63,360 inches, or 1 mile in real life.

Online maps provide easy access to a lot of different kinds of information.

36

CHAPTER 5

Online Maps

Maps that are drawn, kept, and used only online are different from printed maps. Paper maps, once printed, do not change. But online maps are designed to change for each person. An online map user doesn't rely on a cartographer to choose what is or isn't shown. Instead, the user calls up the information she wants. Another difference is that an online map doesn't exist outside of the Internet unless the user prints a copy.

 The first Internet atlas went online in 1994.

Online maps can easily be updated when nations change their borders, become part of other nations, or are newly created.

Levels of Information

An online atlas provides a huge amount of information. For one thing, it may hold thousands of maps, far more than any print atlas. That's just the beginning. A single online map provides a gateway to many levels of information. Click a mouse or tap a touch screen, and a plain map changes to show things such as railroad tracks, rainfall, or high-crime areas.

Google Earth

The online globe Google Earth appeared in 2005. It used pictures taken from satellites, aircraft, and other sources to map almost the entire earth in photographs. Since then, Google Earth has expanded what it can do. Today, it provides three-dimensional views of some major cities. A user can go on a ground level road tour of thousands of places. And one click takes users to maps on special subjects such as climate change.

Changing in Real Time

Computer technology also allows organizations to display maps that change in real time. The Doppler radar maps found on many news sites track minute-by-minute changes in the weather. The U.S. Geological Survey Web site shows the location and seriousness of earthquakes around the world. With a click, a user can see quake information from the last 10 minutes, the last 100 years, or almost any other time period.

Hurricanes and other major storms can be tracked on Doppler radar maps.

40

Taking a look at current traffic conditions can help a user decide the best route to take.

From Where to There

Google Maps, MapQuest, and other online mapping sites make it easy to find directions. By typing in a starting point and an end point, a user learns the shortest route to where he wants to go. He also finds out how much time the trip will take. A mouse or fingertip even allows a user to trace out alternate routes right on the map. It is also easy to move the maps around to see other places.

Online mapping sites often lack legends.

Some users can access online maps on their phones.

These kinds of online maps have symbols that show restaurants, schools, and other landmarks. Clicking on a landmark in Google Maps or MapQuest opens a separate window with the landmark's address and phone number. Sometimes the window also includes a Web site or a photograph of the location. Other links may provide traffic information or a weather forecast.

Online maps have changed how people find their way around. But reading maps has stayed the same in many ways. Making sense of a map's orientation, scale, and symbols are all starting points, whether you look at a map online or one imprinted in clay. Next time you look at a map, pay attention to its elements. You'll be an expert map reader in no time! ★

A map reader has a lot of maps to choose from when finding the map that meets his needs.

True Statistics

Number of cardinal directions on a compass rose: 4

Date of Ptolemy's birth: Around 90 CE

Century Europeans rediscovered Ptolemy's writings: 15th

Distance between each parallel of latitude: About 69 mi. (111 km)

Degrees of latitude in the Southern Hemisphere: 90

Location of the prime meridian: 0° longitude

Degrees of longitude in the Western Hemisphere: 180

Number of minutes in 1 degree of latitude or longitude: 60

Number of seconds in 1 minute of latitude or longitude: 60

Date John Harrison finished his prize-winning sea chronometer: 1759

Number of inches in a mile: 63,360

Did you find the truth?

(F) Meridians are always the same distance apart.

(T) The equator separates the Northern and Southern Hemispheres.

Resources

Books

Cooke, Tim, ed. *Maps and Cities*. New York: Gareth Stevens Publishing, 2010.

Lanier, Wendy. *Maps*. Detroit: Thomson Gale, 2008.

Oleksy, Walter G. *Mapping the World*. New York: Franklin Watts, 2002.

Visit this Scholastic Web site for more information on reading maps:
★ www.factsfornow.scholastic.com
Enter the keywords **Reading Maps**

Important Words

cartographer (kahr-TAH-gruh-fur) — a person who makes maps

chronometer (krah-NAH-meh-tur) — an instrument that measures time with great accuracy

compass rose (KUHM-puhs ROZE) — a map element that shows direction

coordinates (koh-OR-duh-nits) — a set of numbers used to show the position of a point on a map

hemispheres (HEM-i-sfeerz) — both halves of the earth

latitude (LAT-i-tood) — the distance north or south of the equator, measured in degrees

longitude (LAHN-ji-tood) — the distance east or west of the prime meridian, measured in degrees

navigator (NAV-i-gate-uhr) — a person in charge of finding where a ship or other vehicle is and how to get it where it needs to go

orientation (or-ee-uhn-TAY-shuhn) — the position of something or the direction something faces

parallel (PAR-uh-lel) — staying the same distance from each other without crossing or meeting

projection (pruh-JEK-shuhn) — a way of representing the globe on a flat page

Index

Page numbers in **bold** indicate illustrations

About the Author

Kevin Cunningham has written more than 40 books on disasters, the history of disease, Native Americans, cartography, and many other topics. Cunningham lives near Chicago with his wife and their young daughter.